Foreword

When asked what I think of when I think of my mother's life, the first word that comes to mind is powerful. Every time someone is asked who they look up to or who motivates them in life, the typical thing to say is your mother, but that could not be truer for me. Watching my mother's life has taught me more than I could ever learn sitting in a class or reading some old history book. My mother's life has taught me that I have no excuse to fail. Every time I get stressed out and feel like giving up, I sit back and think of how little my problems truly are, compared to what my mother has gone through to get to point she's at in life. She's had almost all of the odds against her. She's had every reason to believe there isn't a God and to believe she wasn't meant to be anything in life. Yet her faith in God remains strong. And her success in her career has just begun. I used to have doubts on whether or not there was a God but now I see there's no way there can't be. I look at all He has done in my mother's life and I thank Him every day. Sometimes I wonder how she does it all. She goes to work, events, church, and still has time for my sisters. She's always taught me to give back and help others. There's not been a time I've walked past anyone in need without helping; that's because of her. Without knowing it, every mistake she's ever made or problem she's ever overcome, has helped me grow as a woman. She's taught me so much.

~Alexus A. Gantt

This is dedicated to:

Alexus, Shy'Aire, Lyric, and Nazhaeya, you have been my driving force; and because you call me mom - I'll never give up. Thank you, for always believing in me! I Love you all - to God!

To the city of Reading, Pennsylvania; I thank you for it all – the good, the bad, & the ugly.

Bethany Children's Home & Ms. Naomi Robertson; thanks for giving kids like me a safe place to call home.

The Robinson's; thank you for taking me in and making me part of the family. Thank you for always keeping your doors opened and phone numbers the same – even when I called collect, lol. Thank you for your prayers and for teaching me the importance of prayer. I'm forever grateful for your love and acceptance - and special thanks to Grandma for the food whenever I pull up!!

Mom and Dad; it was a journey, but I understand. I thank you, and I wouldn't trade either of you for the world (you either PopPop James). I love you, unconditionally.

My brothers: Duane, Brian, Darren, Jeff, and Preston; thanks for always having my back while somehow convincing me that I'm a superhero.

My only sister Tanya; you give me courage when I have none (and convo's that self destruct–lol).

My nieces, nephews, and two Godsons

Special regards to my late Grandfather Rev. Roger Lee Henshaw – I truly believe I've got a piece of your heart.

My maternal grandmother and all of my aunts, uncles, and cousins

&

My remaining friends and family,

I love you all and am thankful for your support!!

The Common Factor

I think the one thing most people have in common, regardless of age, race, or religion, is the genuine desire to be happy. People spend much of their lives trying to find something to live for, a genuine purpose - an overall sense of peace. Lifting every rock, opening every book, buying candles and oils; hoping a magic genie grants just one wish or God responds to that one prayer and WAH LAH..... Life is good.

We wear ourselves down through the search and oddly enough I think that's when we find it; when we're tired, broken, weathered, and alone.

Suicidal Thoughts

I remember being about twelve years old; sitting in the back room of the trailer my mom was renting, and wanting to die. I hated my life. I didn't get along with my mom and didn't know my dad. I didn't have any real friends and I felt completely alone. I remember thinking God was a fraud. All those Sunday school classes and old school hymns proclaiming how great God was. What "great God" would give me a life so miserable? How had the "all knowing God" forgotten me?

I would come home from school wondering if anyone would even notice if I was gone. However, up to that point, I hadn't mustered up the courage to make myself disappear. But this day, this day was different. I grabbed a razor from the bathroom and began racing the plastic part up and down my arm, then the blade across my wrist. I truly wanted to die, I didn't want to feel any more pain. I didn't want to hurt my brothers – I didn't want them to find me.

I don't remember much of what happened next but I do remember mom having me admitted into a mental institution. North Western Institute? Yea, something like that.

For the next few years, I went back and forth from home to group homes and foster care pretty fluidly. During one of my moments at home, I was sitting on the living room recliner watching tv with my brothers when my mom asked me to do the dishes. I was zoned off, into whatever the show was, as I told her that I wanted to take a shower first. Because, well you know, in the trailer park washing dishes would use all the hot water. She and I argued - but not for long. Within moments, my mom was standing in front of me with a metal rod. Then swinging, hitting me so hard the recliner flipped over with me in it. I don't remember much of what happened next. I'd passed out with a gash to the head. It was at that moment...*I died*.

Something in me definitely died that day. When I woke up under the recliner, it was all a fog. I didn't know what to do *so I ran*. I was running not knowing where I was going, afraid of where I had been, and what was to come. I remember thinking something had to be really wrong with me, why was I hard to love? At the least, most people are loved by their parents, right? That day I wished I were dead...*I already was.*

ON-5194

I woke up one morning, January 2004, and dropped my three daughters off at school/daycare. I was headed to a court hearing for my daughter's father. He and I had been together for about 6 years, and though most of the women in the city knew him about as intimately as I did, he was all I knew of love...*and I was a rider*. We'll refer to him as N.B.

N. B. was a good guy with a great heart; a heart almost as big as his desires for other women and he had a way of living that was even bigger...but that's his story to tell.

On this day, I was going to court to support him...*I told y'all I was a rider*. He had been charged with two separate incidents, and if found guilty, N.B. was looking at a lot of time. The court hearing was getting ready to start, and my best friend and I had just sat down. Not too long after, I made eye contact with the investigator assigned to his case. I immediately felt uneasy. I turned to my friend and said "he's gonna arrest me." She thought I was trippin'. I mean, I didn't have any warrants or anything but when you're living a certain lifestyle, you can kinda sense when it's about to go down. I watched - on the low, as the investigator got up and left the courtroom. At that point I tapped my friend nervously, suggesting we leave too. As I stood to walk out the court room, my heart was in my throat; and as the courtroom doors opened, all hell broke loose. There stood officers brandishing guns with handcuffs in hand.

The investigator had decided to charge me with conspiracy to commit attempted murder along with dozens of other charges. I reached towards my pocket and the officers yelled for me to stop, "put your hands where we can see them!" At that point it was all a blur. I could hear them but nothing was registering. I reached deeper into my pocket and without further warning that was it...*I died that day*.

The officers rushed me and put me in handcuffs. I don't remember everything that happened next. I don't know if I was that high or that far removed from reality.

As I sat in the cell hour after hour, day after day, waiting to get out of quarantine - time seemed to merge. I could hear the "neighbors" yelling about one drummed up emergency or the other; and when it was quiet, I would try to sleep. Only to be awakened by the sounds of my cellie going through heroine withdrawals.

Some days later I made it to the block, general population. I was able to make phone calls. That's where I discovered that no one was helping with this $100k bail. And though I wasn't guilty of the charges, not a soul seemed to believe me. I mean, nobody in jail is guilty (let them tell it), especially not in the county jail.

Truth was, no one gave a damn about my sob story and street cred didn't amount to anything in terms of collateral. So, *I was stuck*. The mail began to pour in: eviction letters from my landlord and custody documents from my daughter's grandmother and my other daughter's father. The days were long and the nights were longer, but there was no point in trying to end them early. I was on prescribed medication to sleep and they checked under my tongue every time I took it to make sure it went down before I walked away. Sons of.......couldn't even OD in peace!

The county had me in a choke hold...and I couldn't *tap out*.

December 2007, Muncy State Correctional Institution

I was calloused, hopeless, and all out of options. My body was present but lifeless and my heart was cold. I hated my life and didn't much care for anyone else's either. And I'm quite sure and this point, no one gave a damn how I felt. I had emotionally, mentally, and physically damaged so many lives I couldn't even sleep at night. The nightmares would wake me up long before count. I had four daughters, and the thought of them scattered from Pennsylvania to Georgia was like a parasite to my soul.

I was in a cell and, when alone, it was quiet - *deathly quiet*. For the first time in a long time I was forced to deal with me and that was an opponent I hadn't prepared for. Alone in my thoughts was a scary place to be. Flashes of my life would torment me; silhouettes of the people that hurt me, and the people I hurt – danced in the shadows of the night. I would remember the dead bodies I'd seen, last looks and final goodbyes. Etched in my memories was a list of those who were no longer here but were somehow still attached to my soul. I'd have reminiscent pop ups of the abuse I endured; with the shallow voice in my head reminding me that I would never be enough. I was nothing. I would never be anything. Everything I touched - ruined. Even I had to admit it; I was *better off dead*. This was my own personal hell and I created it.

Broken Glass - Stained

Weak, I fell to my knees sobbing; screaming out in years of pain. I hoped that some of what I felt would jolt someone into finally putting me out of my misery. I was tired; exhausted...I didn't have the strength to go on. My body felt like a shell as I laid there weeping; my soul seemed to have *checked out* long ago & I didn't even have enough energy left to summons it back..... So I did what I could.

I laid there and died.

At that moment I felt a sensation; difficult to put into words – it was a feeling. It was peace and purity, genuine and wholesome; it filled every void and warmed every corner of my being. I'd equate it to what a baby must feel the first time he or she rests in their mothers arms. Hearts beating in unison, this feeling was life's harmony. I can't explain it as anything other than love. It was as if someone had wrapped their arms around me, quietly soothing and comforting me - assuring me that everything would be alright. This was unlike anything I'd ever felt before, I couldn't touch it but I could feel it. I was alone – together, with something....... someone. It was there and it was real. I kept my eyes closed because I feared that when I opened them whoever, whatever was comforting me; would disappear, and I needed this.

Finally, the opportunity to completely fall apart; to quit, give up and give in! I needed to be able to be vulnerable; to scream out in pain that life wasn't fair! My childhood should have been better! I deserved to feel love! To know it, undoubtedly! To give it, with no regard! I needed someone to remind me that I was enough! I was smart enough! I was strong enough! I was good enough! That I was not just the sum of my mistakes! And nothing I did would make me too bad to love! I was broken but not destroyed!! I had messed up royally but my crown still awaits me! I was impure and tainted – scattered and in disarray but I was a beautiful disaster!! I was selected; an imperfect canvas to the Greatest artist of all time; and like stained glass – when the light shines through, *I'd become a beautiful masterpiece.*

Spiritual Kaleidoscope

I was in a matrix that showed me screenshots of my life. When I ran away as a child with my head injured, crying and alone, it was God that protected me. He kept me covered and even when I questioned His existence, He never strayed. When I suffered in silence as an adolescent, accepting the notion that I wasn't good enough; feeling abandoned and unloved by my father – He assured me that He is my true father, and He would never forsake me. All the shame that I carried for how badly I behaved was lifted. The tears I held inside as I reflected over every wasted opportunity, I could release now. Through Him I am forgiven and no record of my wrong is kept! God promised me that if I focused on Him, I would be reborn. I would know my place in His kingdom; and no matter what occurred in this world, I would have peace! In that moment I knew that every thirst that my spirit longed for would be quenched...but the old me had to *die first*.

So, ***that day, I died.***

I died to myself

I died to my flesh

        My mistakes and my sins,

I died to my lustful desires

        My shame filled and guilt-ridden thoughts,

I died to the notion that I wasn't enough

I died to the idea that anyone had to accept me, acknowledge me, or understand the plan that God had for my life.

I died to my past and asked God to govern my future.

I pronounced **DEAD**, all that I thought I knew and all that I was.

I starved the demon that thought it had my mind and smothered the parts of me that hated myself.

I made a promise to God that even when it got hard - I would keep going.

When wrong was easier, I would do right. And when my past came back to discourage me, I would bind it with His Word.

The old me, was dead.

Because of Him I died. And because of Him I can now truly live.

Covered by His blood; no amount of wrong I'd done could rid me of it.

To the world, my story was over

; BUT GOD

THIS IS ABOUT YOU!

1. What childhood memory are you still holding on to that is hindering your growth?

For those who have experienced abuse in their childhood:

Sometimes the characteristics we use to identify ourselves are based on the lies we were told as children.

Many times we will begin to claim those identifying traits well into our adulthood.

Does any of this sound relative?

2. Growing up, what negative thing were you told about yourself that you still believe today?

Why do you consider this truth?

What positive attribute can you identify that will counteract this negative?

(Ex: My step mother always said I'd never be successful / Today, I have a degree/job/family/good grades etc)

3. What mistakes have you made that you still haven't forgiven yourself for?

Understand that your mistakes don't define you. Everyone makes mistakes, both big and small.

The strength is in admitting you're wrong and doing better moving forward.

Forgive yourself and apologize to other necessary parties.

Today is a new day.

4. What apology do you feel you needed, but were never given?

If the person(s) is still present, take a moment now and write him/her a detailed letter about how you feel – **don't send it**.

Keep the letter until tomorrow this time, and reread it. If you still feel the same at that point, send it off.

If you don't have their address, it's all good; still write the letter(s).

This exercise is not for them, it's for you.

It's your opportunity to free yourself of any ill feelings you may be holding onto, allowing yourself to move on.

Some apologies we may never get and we've got to be ok with that.

5. What parts of you need to die?

-Old Habits?

-Need To Release A Soul Tie or Four?

We all have our "stuff" with us. Some of these things set us apart, but some are hindrances. Identify the parts of you that are holding you captive at your current level, you'll have to get rid of them to advance. (Sometimes these are the things that bother us horribly about someone else)

If you're wondering why you can't get over an ex; look up that soul tie thing I just mentioned. It gets deep. (No pun intended)

6. What are your five best qualities? (Do Not List Anything Physical)

Was that difficult?

 If so, list 5 more!

Get into the practice of uplifting self talk.

 Tell yourself how intelligent you are, how proud you are of your accomplishments; make positive small talk with yourself. Keep the little mean, shaky voice in your head at bay.

7.   What would the people closest to you say that they love the most about you?

Now reach out to the people closest to you and ask them what they love the most about you. Write their responses below. Compare them with your answers above.

PLACE YOUR HAND HERE WITH MINE

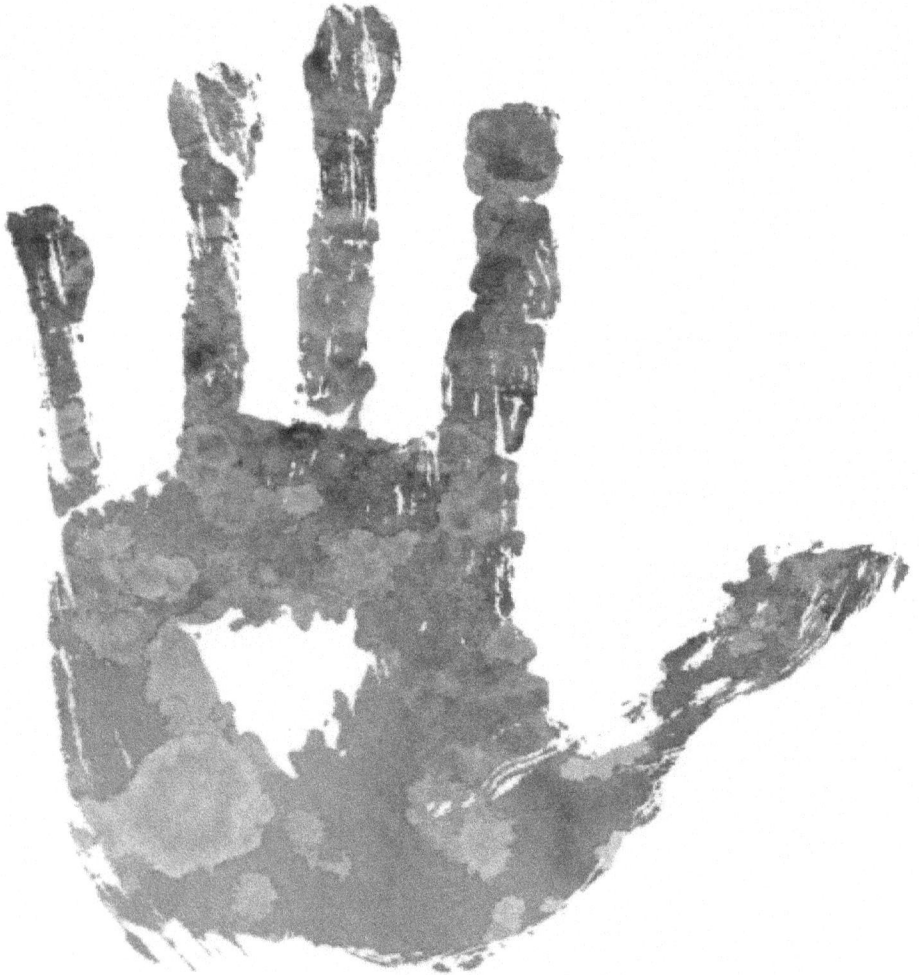

In **Matthew 18:20** (KJV) The bible says,

"Where two or three are gathered together In My name, there am I in the midst of them."

So today, I pray with you. I pray that God free you from anything holding you back. That His love covers and protects you from the harms of this world and any harm you may bring upon yourself. I pray that today the old you passes away so that the new you can live a more fulfilled life. I pray for your peace, your happiness, understanding, and love. I pray that God guides you and that from this point forward you never lose your way. Your best life is in every day that follows.

In Jesus' name AMEN.

8. TAKE THE OATHE!

Today the old me has died. In his/her place, there's a new me; full of life and limitless possibilities. Today, I don't have time for negative thoughts or negative people. I'm focused on my goals and look forward to better days.

_____

SIGN HERE

A word from the author:

Just so we're clear on what I mean when I reference "death" and "dying" or to "kill" a part of my or your self - I mean to take breath from. Proclaiming that we are no longer breathing life into anything that isn't good for us; no longer allowing negative situations to take up precious space in our future. So though physically we are still pretty much the same; spiritually, mentally, emotionally, we are refreshed and ready to start new lives. When you reemerge as a child of God, who you used to be no longer exists...the old you is dead; and the new you has just begun to understand what living truly means. As you continue your walk you'll begin to see......there is not room for both the old you and the new you in your life; ultimately, the choice is always yours.

Special thanks to:

CoreyJon; for all of the pushing, encouraging, and believing in me; for the late night spell checks and CAFÉ BUSTELLO, I appreciate you! "Don't tell me what to do" lol

Tati and the crew; thanks for never making me feel like anything less than part of the family.

Draya; I watched you in videos from prison and said "she's from my hood." Every time I saw you rise, it encouraged me to keep going. You have done it your way and your hustle is impeccable.

The Caddy's; I can't say enough how thankful I am for your friendship and love. #MJsGodMa

MeMa and DJ; thank you both for being "grandmothers" to my babies, you are the village. (Hey Sis)

Charlamagne; YO! You always made me feel like I could be and do whatever the f.....lol. Thanks for accepting my random pop up trip to NY! Thanks for being a mentor. For putting together a dope book that lit a fire under me to get my first one done! And for allowing me to host your book tour here in The Met; that was real.

DJ BLORD; from day one your hustle felt like passion in human form. You've never said a word to me that I couldn't use to grow......think about that. Salute!

Michelle, DeeDee, Stevie the 3peat! Keish!! Chris C. thanks for hiring a felon! BJ Murphy-You DA MAN!

DT; you've been there from day 1, supporting and pushing me to level up. Thanks for having my back!

Deon and Neiko; you have both been "no men" but always with love. For your ear(s), your prayers, your advice, your friendship. Thank you! ....waddup Puff?!

Temp, Ris, Mel, Jigga, LeeLee, Shan, Baybe; I Love ya'll! Bunchie; shut up! Robert; thanks for being a co-parent and friend...hey Robin, Bert, Sue, Whitney, Pete, Randy, Fern, and W.Mel. YO, James! HIM JONES!! BCH-Crystal & Lisa! Rashaun Green!!! R.Peterson & family-you inspire me. Camille-ourlittlebigdreams.com!! #BabySho thank your mom for encouraging me! J from MIA in TX waddup!

Nature & Quis; salute! JoJo, Pam, Robbie, HVidal, Mel (Y.H.), Johnny V, Chizo, Z, Gov, Chris, Hutch, Fatz, Jenn, Jackie, Roxxy, Trix, Dog, Sip, P YAGGA – salute to you all. To the old Legion crew, Kerry-Talia-Sissy-Jeanette- get ready for the book signing! Tara & Taj keep leading by example.

Thank you to my LA Pastor, Pastor Toure'Roberts; those Youtube videos keep me going! To Pastor Kelvin Smith at Steele Creek Church of Charlotte, you're a blessing to us all! Kim Burnette, thank you!

To anyone I missed; blame my head - not my heart. Your support means a lot. THANK YOU!

Tyson, I did it ☺

www.ingramcontent.com/pod-product-compliance
Lightning Source LLC
Chambersburg PA
CBHW060608030426
42337CB00019B/3670